ON QUARRY BEACH

ALSO BY ROBERT JAGGS-FOWLER

Fiction

Lamplight in the Shadows

Poetry

A Journey with Time

Non-fiction

The Law and Medicine: Friend or Nemesis?

To Richard,
With best wishes,
Robert [illegible]

ON QUARRY BEACH

COLLECTED POEMS 2008–2013

ROBERT JAGGS-FOWLER

Matador
9 Priory Business Park,
Wistow Road, Kibworth Beauchamp,
Leicestershire. LE8 0RX
Tel: 0116 279 2299
Email: books@troubador.co.uk
Web: www.troubador.co.uk/matador
Twitter: @matadorbooks

ISBN 978 1788033 107

British Library Cataloguing in Publication Data.
A catalogue record for this book is available from the British Library.

Printed and bound in the UK by TJ International, Padstow, Cornwall
Typeset in 11pt Aldine401 BT by Troubador Publishing Ltd, Leicester, UK

Matador is an imprint of Troubador Publishing Ltd

FSC www.fsc.org
MIX
Paper from responsible sources
FSC® C013056

To the memory of the many who have unwittingly influenced my thinking, but are no longer here for me to say 'thank you'. May you rest in peace and rise in glory.

INTRODUCTION AND ACKNOWLEDGEMENTS

All the poems within this, my second collection of poetry, were written between the years 2008 to 2013. As with *A Journey with Time*, the poems are eclectic in both their subject matter and style. The only common denominator has been the perpetual tolerance of my wife, Linda, who has shouldered the long periods of my introverted solitude and silence with great patience, and for which I am most grateful.

A note in respect to a few of the poems:

'My Neighbour's Lawn' won the Fathom Prize for Poetry in 2010, and was included in the anthology *Fathom 10* (Barton upon Humber: Fathom Press, 2010). 'Haiku from the Caribbean' was shortlisted in the *Writing Magazine* Sea Poetry Competition in December 2010, with the judge commenting that it "only just missed final placing".

'An Intermezzo for Love' was included in the anthology *What is Love?* (London: United Press Ltd, 2011).

‘End of the Line’ was influenced by Adam Scott Rote’s painting ‘Writer’s Block’, which can be viewed at: http://tinyurl.com/zz8sf3t

‘The Artist and the Dancer’ was influenced by the artist Gary Welton, whose work can be viewed at: www.garywelton.com

I have previously written elsewhere that a poem is the capture and subsequent distillation of a moment, a thought, or an experience, into its essential components. It is an emotion’s purest form as sensed and understood by the eye, mind and heart of the poet. Poems can therefore be very personal and treasured; but like all valuable gifts, they need to be shared to achieve their full value. In this collection, I offer a few of my own distilled moments, and I hope that you can also glimpse the magic behind them.

ROBERT M. JAGGS-FOWLER
Barton upon Humber
January 2017

www.robertjaggsfowler.com

CONTENTS

2010

2011

2008

DAWN ON THE GANGES

As day's golden orb rises in the east,
and vermillion rays illuminate
the steep stepped shores patrolled by holy beast,
Hindu's pujas assist the hand of fate.
Whilst warm grey waters lap where women bathe,
and smoke obscures the white-robed men whose sight
is blind to wooden boats and temples save
the burning pyres of loved ones' final rites,
dead spirits rise led by a soaring kite,
the knot of night again unfolds to day,
bright lotus flowers open to the light,
and coloured saris turn the grey to gay.
As deities respond to sacred acts,
life's circle turns upon these ancient ghats.

AN INDIAN PERSPECTIVE (1)

A splash of water
stirs a dusty river bed.
The monsoon begins.

ESTIMATING THE ULTIMATE

Does human life have value as of right?
Or is that right a part of fiscal might?
Who decides which attributes carry worth?
Or is our price fixed at the time of birth?

Is value dependent on creed or race?
Is one worth more if in a state of grace?
If that is so, then who decides one's judge?
Can one man's strength negate a nation's grudge?

Does life's agenda dictate mankind's fee?
Do morals, love and freedom hold the key?
What then of lands time has long forgot?
When is the potter equalled by the pot?

Can humankind ascribe a common law:
that the rich must be servants to the poor?
The world must keep perspective well in sight;
for all lives should hold value as of right.

AN INDIAN PERSPECTIVE (2)

From the riverbank,
plumes of white-grey smoke ascend.
The cremation ends.

SUNSET IN JODHPUR

Shadows lengthen,
as a reddening western sky
enfolds the light of day.

Fragrance of jasmine.

A gold adorned
rich tapestry of colour,
with life's liquor
cranially borne in
unsupported earthen pot,
walks amidst a rising grey cloud
stirred by cloven hooves.

Personifying dignity and grace,
the gwali turns for home.

THE REMEMBRANCE DAY PARADE

As he walked up to the rostrum,
silence round him fell;
and whilst he gazed upon the steadfast ranks,
emotive lines began to tell.

Too many lives were lost before today:
young men and women – yesterday's youth.
They were the cheques we drew to pay
for the blinded search for fallacious truth.

You are the inspired; the fortunate few
who have lived through to this day:
the ones who now must tell the world
to find a better way.

It is the charge of those who live
beyond vanquished dreams of many men,
to find the strength to forgive;
to learn and love as best you can.

And in so doing, let us ensure
a sense of remembrance, not of rage;
may this quietude beyond the war
turn pugnacious soldier into reflective sage.

Thus, he stood upon the rostrum as
the silence round him fell,
and gazed upon the steadfast ranks
of those returned from hell.

2009

AN ELEGY FOR RURAL LIFE

There's snow in the folds of Buttertub Heights,
and wind in the hills that is blowing mean.
Though ice lines the ridge where the kites take flight,
hamlets lie warm between blankets of green.
The scene's one unaltered from yesteryear,
or so it would seem when viewed from afar:
dry stone walls protecting those dear from fear;
none foreseeing the dangers brought by car.
Where once the church bell tolled for passing day,
the vicarage is now prefixed by 'Old'
and, usurping times eulogised by Gray,
sale boards proclaim lives that cannot be sold.
Modernity has through the dale progressed,
and all once revered has been laid to rest.

SECULAR COMMUNION

The cold, crisp crunch of
frost underfoot
voices the village's
shivering, Sabbath stillness.

Led by a mechanised, melodic toddler,
a familial trio approaches; oblivious
to the exhortations of
a distant tolling bell:

a duo of triumvirates disunited.

Forced off the kerb by
a persuasive swerve of the tricycle,
I smile at the battle cry; my amusement
parentally captured, magnified, returned.

Behind, the rhetorical refrain continues its
erratic, pioneering course:
'Happy birthday to you,
happy birthday to you, happy birthday…'

THE WATERFALL PARADOX

Melt water arcs and plunges;
a maelstrom of crystal arrows freed
from their limestone quiver.
Ancient boughs distort
amidst the mirror's shattered remnants.

White water,
white foam,
white noise.

Rays of equinoctial sunshine
scavenge the icy carnage,
oblivious to the whispering breeze
mixing odours of damp moss and wild garlic:
medicaments for nature's battered tranquillity.

Assiduous,
annotative,
assimilating:

I absorb the rooks' cawing bass accompaniment;
the chaffinch's recitative: a duet
superimposed upon the aqueous chorus,
for a celandine audience, beneath
this amphitheatre's cerulean dome.

Surreptitiously,
subliminally,
sublimely,

I am clandestinely subsumed by nature's forces:
autonomy replaced by omni-directional,
primeval signals of life's supremacy. I am
reduced to a conduit amidst existential machinery;
an inconsequential piece of time's jigsaw, yet

alive,
empowered,
omniscient.

A METAPHYSICAL CONVERSATION WITH MY FATHER

Today
was once your future;
my reality
cherished dreams of your past.
Time conspired with Fate;
the baton transferred;
history written.

I thirst
for tomorrow's knowledge,
certain that,
until life's orb sinks
into the sea of permanent night,
it remains for me
to be what you might have been.

Fuelled
by deep draughts of your
exhaled dreams,
I aspire
to be everything and more

you wished to be,
lest I drown in my ignorance.

Yet, I am
greater than life's accumulated past.
The weight I bear,
mankind's destiny fashioned
by actions of yesteryear,
is a transient load
of distrustful relevance.
For I have
my own direction for tomorrow;
understanding
that great people are
commonplace men,
motivated
by extraordinary souls.

And therein is
enlightenment.
For your yesterday's tomorrow
eventually blends with my future's past.
The baton will exchange again;
inspiration will renew,
as Today is born

anew.

MEDICAL RECEIVERSHIP

'Six months...'

A hollow echo of my earlier words:
part statement, part question;
a verbal search for meaning.

Before us a computer serves
as the silent spokesperson, for
the jury of blood tests and scans;
behind, a wall clock ticks with
darkened emphasis.

His eyes return to mine,
probe for a chink of hope,
and find none.

Six months
to close a lifetime.

A LADIES' NIGHT MUSING

I cannot here pretend to understand
the enigma of nature's upper hand;
those possessed of a labyrinthine mind,
in which potential suitors usually find
themselves lost within a feminine haze:
nature's own indecipherable maze.

When Adam fell beneath the spell of Eve
could he have begun to conceive that,
upon the world, his actions would fling
a conundrum designed henceforth to bring
male descendants immeasurable strife:
how to comprehend the gift of a wife?

Now, it's true that wives don't begin as such;
but the youngest of ladies has as much
of that air of mystery they portray,
which incessantly deepens from the day
of their wedding; then henceforth to perplex
the wisest of the opposite sex.

Of course, there is no riddle of why
men stay, forever seeking ways to buy
their way into favour; it's clear to see
when surrounded by a sea of beauty.
Radiance in abundance; gorgeous gems;
exquisite wit, charm, and a few raised hems.

Intelligent, calculating and quick:
these ladies know full well what makes men tick.
Household chores sorted, mealtimes trouble-free;
overspent credit card? Now let us see...
a spot of romance – it's really quite simple
how he relents at the sight of a dimple.

Whether it is the prettiness of youth
or the serene beauty of age, the truth
is that men succumb to their loveliness,
compliant to their every whim. Yes!
Potent is the daughter, wife or lover,
and ne'er misjudge the power of one's mother!

So, when we appraise the gift of Adam,
shallow we'll be, whilst trying to fathom
a truth we are destined never to ken.
Yet, resolute is the culture of men.
On the crease we'll fall – we'll ne'er cease the fight,
as we flutter like moths around her light.

THE NOVICE

Slow down, that's much too quick, dear,
and please, do not tongue my ear;
just get on and do the deed for which you've paid.
It is clear you've drunk some beer;
did you need to quench your fear?
I can tell this is the first time you've been laid.

Try unfastening from the right:
do you need a little light?
Yes, you'll find one on the side within its foil.
I can't make out your mumblings:
let me help with your fumblings;
go carefully there, you're pressing on my boil.

Of course, but listen, honey,
such service costs more money.
Have you thought about the option that you're gay?
I think you're nowhere near, sir,
so, it's time for us to stir, sir;
I wish you better luck another day.

2010

THREE SCORE YEARS LESS TEN

The man has turned fifty.
Half a century of achievement
gazes from the mirror:
well-lettered, a little creased,
edges flecked by a whitened patination:
intriguing footnotes and addendums;
sporadic revisions to the first edition.

Probing eyes absorb the jacket.

Not quite contemporary, the
title remains undiminished.
A promising work in progress:
a curious mix of genre and form;
part novel, part scholarly treatise,
with poetry greeting prose.

The question is perceived but unspoken.

Five decades of prequel are mentally rifled:
musical annotation interlaced with romance.
The pages following are pristine,

void of script and pagination.
The reflection smiles and nods:
the understanding complete.

The man has turned fifty,
and the swallows are amassing…

ABOVE WESTMINSTER BRIDGE

(After *Upon Westminster Bridge*
by William Wordsworth, 1802)

Who could have dreamt two hundred years ago,
that far above this bridge, within the sky,
would rise a wheel known as the London Eye;
whose bespoked pods hoist eager voyeurs to
a view surprising e'en the flying crow?
Where ships, Westminster and a gherkin by
St Paul's, with royal residences vie
with spans, whose arches intimately know
the flowing waters of the Thames (grey tides
immune to fluctuations of the State).
Lured by this serpentine flow, three eyes guide
today's poet to all that still lends weight.
Now vibrant; eschewing rest; this city
wears modernity with sage majesty.

THE ENIGMA OF WIND TURBINES

Atop the region's highest crest, they stand,
white, tri-limbed sentinels; skeletal clones.
Mute communicants between sky and land,
they convert power against public ohms.
Acolytes to the force of rushing air,
they wait, with patient arms outstretched, to seize
cold north winds or autumnal squalls that dare
disturb the pleasing spring or summer breeze.
Aeolus, Storm God and son of Hellen,
dreamt of such tools with the might to induce
Anemoi into static rebellion:
wind competing with the charges of Zeus!
What will future archaeologists say
about these pagan temples built today?

MEALTIMES EN VACANCES

When is breakfast just breakfast,
when it's really time for lunch?
And if that glass of wine is made to last,
one begins to get the hunch
that it's 'time for tea, I reckon'.
Hence, neatly stretch the hours
until evening cocktails beckon:
'Will that be two brandy sours?'

Thus, a lazy day at last is through,
as we wend our way to dinner;
And that is how our waistlines grew,
with no hope of getting slimmer!

MY NEIGHBOUR'S LAWN

has a black scar:
eight feet by six;
four inches deep.
Burgeoning black bags
sit stacked by
the remnants of a spoil heap.

Glinting against
this dark excavation
is a silver tablespoon.

Improbable;
but then,
my brother once cut
our lawn
with a pair of scissors.

UPON THE CARIBBEAN SEA

I am listening to the sound of lapping waves:

the original music of millennia past;
preceding man and beast, tree and flower;
before mountain range or valley floor;
a wind-borne voice from Earth's birth.

As each wave crests, and falls, and crests again,
the language of God echoes from the start of time.

HAIKU FROM THE CARIBBEAN

Wave laps against wave:
wind's primeval voice echoes
from the start of time.

AN INTERMEZZO FOR LOVE

Draw back the curtains of the night;
prolong the beauty of twilight.
May the crimson skies once more show,
reflected in the moon's soft glow,
the softness of your features fair,
enhanced by joy; devoid of care.

And when, at last, the dark descends,
let love's embraces make amends
for all perceptions of neglect.
Then, let sleep come without regret,
bringing dreams devoid of sorrow;
recharging minds for tomorrow

such that, when the dawn once more breaks,
a new love for each other wakes;
empowering hearts to seize the day
and, all deeds done, once more to say:
draw back the curtains of the night;
prolong the beauty of twilight...

LIGHTS

Green was the light on the doctor's car,
casting ghostly reflections in the snow-clad night.
Blue was the addition the ambulance crew brought,
as they fought for his life with technical might.
White was the light he had seen through his pain,
as he momentarily surfaced, before going again.
But black was the light of the undertaker's hearse;
as it will be evermore in my universe.

WINTER

Two collared doves sit
huddled on a snow-clad branch,
dreaming of springtime.

AN EX-PAT'S LAMENT

(With apologies to Robert Browning)

Oh, to be in England
now that winter's there;
for, whilst you freeze in England,
think of me and have a care.
There, the deciduous trees are leafless,
whilst chill, northern winds blow, I guess;
and robins sit, fluffed up, on snowy boughs
in England – now!

And after Guy Fawkes Night, Christmas follows:
when, with mulled wine and mistletoe, sorrows
are forgotten around crackling log fires;
whilst children give snowmen carrot noses,
and carols are sung in the streets by choirs
stamping cold feet; their ears red as roses.
I miss steamy windows, and candlelight,
and the hoar frost that forms in the night.
I yearn to wear coats and scarves made of wool,
or dress in Black Tie for a winter's ball.
Choosing this Mediterranean heat
against England's seasons is bitter sweet.

2011

A PHYSICIAN-POET'S PLATITUDES

Trust me, I'm a poet;
I've not an ill word in my head.
I will not weave seductive lines
to get into your bed.

Pure will be my sonnets
proclaiming your feminine charm.
My sestinas and villanelles
will ne'er do any harm.

But if one day my hands should stray
whilst we share a mocha,
I'll keep my strongest line to last:
Trust me, I'm a doctor!

HAIKU FROM A SMALL ISLAND

Horizontal rain
driven by Atlantic gales:
summer on Lundy.

KEEPERS OF THE NORTH LIGHT

(The North Light on Lundy Island, built by Trinity House in 1897, was automated in 1991. A narrow-gauge manually operated railway once assisted the keepers in moving supplies from the cliff to the lighthouse.)

The tracks now lie abandoned,
resigned to a rusting sleep;
with ghosts of ancient mariners
the sole company left to keep.

I've walked between these rails,
on that well-worn path you trod;
feeling your wind-ravaged presence
in every sea-sprayed sod.

And I've marvelled at your lives
amidst these rock-strewn shores,
battling ferocious weather
to save ships from Neptune's jaws.

A winch, not turned for decades;
cliff-face steps, worn down like broken teeth;

a cannon, no longer fired when bound by fog
to warn of dangers far beneath.

Now, the light is automated,
with no need for humankind;
but the artefacts of history
ensure you're not lost from mind.

ON QUARRY BEACH

That day dawned.
Dark leaden skies held a golden promise,
and so, we went.

Laden with a back-packed feast,
we trod the goat path to Three-quarter Wall,
down to Quarry Pond and up
to the old time-keeper's hut, which now
keeps nothing but F.G.'s memory.

The descent started there.
A steep winding path,
part stone, part grass,
led through shoulder-high bracken
nestling with yellow-flowering gorse,
before arriving at the final roped descent
to four wooden steps
and a rock-strewn beach,
with no exit save the sea or retreat.

There we sat,
pondering fresh, green fronds of seaweed

swirling at the water's edge
against a backdrop of rounded boulders
smoothed by eons of wind and waves;
reminiscing with every sun-flecked lapping wave,
as the years rolled back, until
time itself stood insignificantly still.

And there,
on Quarry Beach,
we understood all we needed to know;
and yet knew nothing,
except that which had drawn us there,
together...

UPON GALLOWS HILL, LUNDY

A tumulus upon the eastern coast
holds court to a view few others can boast.
Yet propriety calls for one to stop:
here once was a noose and the hangman's drop.
This tranquil island once abhorred the law;
but if I was a smuggler I am sure,
if I came to find my fates blew ill
such that I had to die upon this hill,
I'd gaze on Hell's Gate and the rocky Rat,
content to breathe my last, 'till that was that.

THE OUTING

A day in Mistress London.

As always,
I succumb to hidden charms,
before slinking back to the Shires
laden with books
and a faint sense of guilt.

A TRANSCULTURAL EXCHANGE

With machine-gun precision,
a burst of resonant drumming escapes
the woodland edge, ricocheting
through the library window.
Formerly engrossed in a book,
I pause to listen.

He has been resident for six weeks now.
The trees have become territorially marked;
reminiscent of a graffiti artist's tags.
Such etchings are prognostic:
tell-tale signs of a tree beyond its prime;
an age-induced, creaking existence.

My joints are like that.
Old and worn, they also creak; a reminder
that I, too, am beyond my prime.
I rise to spy on my new neighbour,
causing a staccato of crepitus
to issue from two arthritic knees.

Across the clearing,
a woodpecker pauses to listen.

HAIKU FROM A REPUBLIC

Throughout Cuban skies
the turkey vultures hover,
waiting for Castro.

I DID NOT SEARCH FOR YOUR NAME

It just appeared in a list of websites
as I Googled another.

Twenty years have passed; yet,
according to the newspaper report,
having returned to
the county of your roots
you did not re-marry,
had no children,
and lived alone with your dog.

You were cremated four days ago
at 1.40pm,
age 47.

THE CLARINET

What made me pause where you lay
open-cased,
rejected amidst the bric-a-brac of
a flea-market stall?
Dry-corked, reed-less;
you exuded the historic aroma
of a thousand smoky nights.
Did I subconsciously heed your soundless call;
hesitating, before stooping to inspect
numerous working parts until satisfied
that your abandonment was premature?

Haggling against the stall-holder's indifference,
you were freed for a ransom of thirty pounds.

Now,
cleansed of your jazz-club patina;
corks greased; mouthpiece loaded with wafered bamboo;
you are re-assembled for the first time in
... how many years?
You inhale the first draught of warm, moist air:

an F follows a C – at first hesitant,
then, at Mozart's behest,
lingering;
the melody's rise and fall hauntingly beautiful as,
from the soul, you sing of your re-birth.

IN THE VALLEY OF THE SHADOW

Driving in those early hours
was a consummate pleasure:
sunlit and empty,
the winding lane stretched unending
into the blue-skied promise
of a glorious summer day.
Flocks of sparrows animated
the sentinel hedgerows,
beyond which lay
gently curvaceous fields strewn with beige bales
punctuating the previous day's progress
of a combine harvester.

A thud,
and a flurry of feathers.

Why,
on such a morning,
did I have to become
the instrument
of your
death?

LIFE

('Doctor, what is the point of life, when it is full of so much strife?')

Life is the taste of ice cream on a summer's day;
the smell of coffee, or new-mown hay;
a storm raging over a Cumbrian fell;
the frothy head on a pint of ale;
a steel band on a Caribbean isle;
climbing a stone wall by way of a stile.

Life is watching condors soar over the Colca Mountains;
throwing coins over a shoulder into the Trevi Fountain;
the rich bouquet of a vintage wine;
the twitch of a salmon upon a line;
watching fruit bats flying at twilight;
hearing an owl hoot at the dead of night.

Life is the amber of whisky in a crystal glass;
the stirring sound of a band of brass;
the bend of trees amidst a winter's gale;
a fall of snow upon a Yorkshire dale;

the peace of an old country churchyard;
an eloquent speech by the English bard.

Life is the sunset over the Mediterranean Sea,
and the gentle hum of a honey bee;
the clink of ice in a glass of gin;
the sensual touch of a lover's skin;
Mozart's concerto for a clarinet;
a library of books, all perfectly set.

Life is a skein of geese in an autumnal sky;
the first bite of a freshly baked apple pie;
an old stone bridge over a tumbling beck;
sipping champagne on a cruise ship's deck;
carols by candlelight at Christmas time;
writing a poem in elusive rhyme.

You ask 'what is the point of life?'
And, though it cannot be devoid of strife,
the answer to me is perfectly clear;
it cannot be plainer put, my dear.
All these and more provide the meaning to life;
take time to look, and you'll find they're rife.
There is no need for a more complex take;
life simply exists for life's own sake.

FORTUNE TELLING IN THE 21ST CENTURY

I can still sense the gravitas of the moment when,
in a room stilled by a collective expectation,
my grandmother prophesised the future.

We would watch her swirling the last drop of tea
three times anti-clockwise before up-ending her cup,
and then wait for an eternity of seconds whilst
the dregs drained and the future formed.

Held breaths were ever so lightly exhaled as she
stared into the porcelain depths, where the pattern of
tea leaves assumed paramount importance.

Forty years on, I lift my mug,
carefully copy the exact memory of her example and,
with a quickening pulse, confront my outlook;
unprepared for the shock of unbroken whiteness.

Ruefully, my gaze turns towards the teapot,
and I wonder which of the two tea bags
has imprisoned the secrets of my destiny.

REMINISCENCES ON A TRAIN

It is raining.
Flecks on the glass become droplets,
coalesce into rivulets, turn horizontally
and gather pace as
the train outraces the rain.

The shower becomes a downpour,
then a storm. Spouts of water
bounce off passing streets; torrents
gush from downpipes, overpowering gutters,
converting roads to rivers. And

with each moment, the scenery changes;
the years roll back, until I sense the
cold, biting wind of a Yorkshire dale;
your hood-framed face smiling through
a curtain of dripping water.

I hear, too, the wind raging around
a cliff-top cottage on Lundy Isle,
as you sip wine by candlelight;
and I sense the humidity as you shower
outside amidst the heat of a Maldivian storm.

With every cloudburst, the dust
of the years is washed away, revealing
memory after memory until the
scene settles on two stone steps
within a Lincoln doorway, framing

an umbrella,
and two people, twenty years younger;
and I know the intensity of that
rain-soaked moment when
I knew…

2012

THE INN AT WHITEWELL

The scene from this aged oaken desk has
probably lain unchanged for centuries;

a green, tree-lined valley, circumscribed
by six interlocking, sun-dappled hills.

Rural perfection, completed at this very moment
by an in-flight of pheasants, a sheep, and

the river's incessant murmuring; all beneath
this ancient manor house's sentient gaze.

White water smooths boulders littering
the river bed; crystal whiteness reflected

by a thin layer of snow-icing adorning
the farthermost hill; an ecological cake,

as though God himself was saying
'Happy birthday; behold, and now make a wish'.

BRIKSDAL

Splintering ice falls.
Magnificent in retreat,
the glacier melts.

GLOBAL WARMING

Melt-water escapes the glacier's edge,
taking refuge in the mountain's fissured rock
to rendezvous with other rivulets,
then emerge as frantic foaming torrents;
white jagged scars that rent the tree-lined slopes,
as, to the sound of thunderous self-applause,
they leap, dive and plunge towards their freedom,
before unleashing to the valley floor
seven thousand years of memories:
lost in an instance amidst the spray and mist.

UNDERSTANDING THE NORWEGIAN PSYCHE

I think that I, too, might become depressed
in a land where colour has been suppressed;
where I awake to see, day after day,
earth, sea and sky in fifty shades of grey.

END OF THE LINE

(In response to the painting *Writer's Block*, by the American artist Adam Scott Rote, and dedicated to Ernest Hemingway)

Everything is still here:

his old typewriter with its rusted keys;
the inevitable whisky glass; complete with amber residue
and the up-ended bottle. Defiantly the finest of malts;
its bouquet long displaced by sea breezes
infiltrating the broken pane.

The dust is new.

Or at least that covering the fallen flakes of paint is new.
Older, accumulated layers long preceded the décor's demise,
cushioning its fall onto the sun-scorched pine table,
where fragments of yesteryear now lay scattered
like discarded words.

Lost and abandoned words;
words lacking ordered meaning;
words fallen from the disused roller that,
but for the want of paper, could
say so much, yet explain so little:

if it wasn't for the keys.

Two keys;
house and car, clinging for security
to the dry, faded leather fob on which
the outline of his initial can still be traced
like a tactile echo; driving

the eye to beyond the window,
where palm trees and a vivid blue sky
contrast with internal decay,
and the gently lapping waves on sand
have long since obliterated his footprints.

THE ARTIST AND THE DANCER

(Dedicated to the American movement artist,
Gary Welton)

Alone, beneath a spotlight
centre-left of an empty stage,
she dances to the music
for an audience in her mind;

whilst, in the shadows of the wings,
a benign voyeur, possessed,
captures her flowing movements
in a brush-stroked pas-de-deux.

Each allonge and pirouette
keeps the artist in his trance,
as he renders to acrylic
complex rhythms of her dance;

until at last she falls exhausted,
and his palette's work is done;
to remain undisturbed upon an easel
for several years to come.

Decades later: a champagne reception
for a gallery's opening night where,
from the shadows, an old man gazes
as a graceful lady stands and sighs

alone, beneath a spotlight,
at a figure centre-left of a canvas stage,
where she now dances for an audience
with music in their minds.

FRAGILE LIVES

How deceptive is the silent water
of deep tranquil lakes of time gone by,
beneath whose surface lies the wreckage
of traumas past, yet ne'er overlooked.

As the thrown stone causes ripples to
spread disruption far and wide,
so too, the thoughtless deed or careless word,
whose murky water laps at distant shores.

Just as the spill of milk annuls its value,
and melting snowflakes revoke their charm,
fading strains of music's final cadence
cannot replay the magic gone before.

No matter how life's potter expertly
toils to repair fragmented pots,
truth dictates it will not hence perform
as once it did before the careless drop.

As a desert's undulating face is changed
by restless grains of time in shifting sands,

so, too, do loathsome episodes demand
old friendships' maps submit to be redrawn.

Whilst a full stop might end a chapter,
and a final chapter will close a book,
in life, joint authors may again conspire
to write a fitting sequel to their plot.

Though fragile lives can be reconstituted,
as past deeds are quietly put to rest,
lessons learned must never be forgotten,
if pain, once raised, is to remain repressed.

THE OLD HOUSE IN VOUNI

Something stirred today
down an ancient cobbled side street,
amidst a deserted mountain village,
where donkey once gave way to donkey,
and the old stone house sits waiting;

abandoned,

save for lizards within its crumbling walls,
and a rambling bougainvillea
whose vines of rose-red petals entwine
levitating balconies, when not securing
paint-peeled shutters or rust-bolted doors.

Communicating two hundred years of history
through a hand upon its façade,
rock dust of eternities passionately vibrated
with inherited Grecian DNA, conjuring
the subliminal picture of a writer's retreat,

where empty rooms echo to
characters' ceaseless chatter

in stories begging to be told, as they dance
amidst filtered beams of sunlight,
or drift on cooling breezes, calling

unsuspecting scribes like sirens
from Homer's *Odyssey*, with promises
of exotic literary journeys, unsurpassed
and irresistible; mantic and romantic tales,
both old and yet to come.

Eventually, leave must be wrestled
from its venerable rustic charm,
but not before unwittingly settling
a guardant portion of enamoured soul,
recumbent in the courtyard's shade,

as a deposit.

UPON WATCHING EUGENE O'NEILL'S PLAY 'LONG DAY'S JOURNEY INTO NIGHT'

Was it
the incessant arguments?

Or the false understanding, closely followed
by barbed and bitter recriminations?
The suffocating concern,
interspersed by accusations and humiliation?

Or perhaps the demand for improvement, revoking
begrudging praise, itself tempered by
a thinly disguised veil of envy?

Maybe the sanctimonious implorations for
sobriety and abstinence, lubricated by whisky
or delivered on a raft of nicotine?

Possibly the assured, prejudiced dogmatism:
uneducated minds closed
to the chance of being mistaken?

Assuredly, the pervading truth that
a shared genetic inheritance
does not guarantee benign complicity,
nor genial accord?

Whichever it was,
the penetrating script touched a nerve;
prodded a tender bruise;
picked at psychological scars.

Unearthing long-forgotten memories
and suppressed emotions,
the play of another's life became
the observer's synonymous biography;
painfully intense,
yet irresistible viewing.

A staged catharsis for a repressed youth.

2013

A LYRICAL POSY

The words come softly,
like gentle rain on a spring morning;
the whisper of a hummingbird's wings;
the murmur of grasses in a summer's breeze;
the touch of a kiss upon reciprocal lips.

They are not hesitant, but searching;
ensuring their choice truly reflects
the intended depth of meaning;
nuances of something exceptional;
secrets gently held in a common bond

between two people.
And they finally settle as the
enduring trio, unsurpassed by countless poets
for the deepest of richness they imbue:
'I love you'.

WASP NEST

Soft and unheralded,
white powder descends, clinging
to the city's elevated façade,
sending workers scurrying for cover;
their lithe bodies leaving a wake of snowy trails.

Concealed within her papery sanctum
the attentive queen mixes proffered
samples with saliva; oblivious to the
unforetold treachery without, or the
deep silence about to descend within.